AdWords Mastery: The Ultimate Guide to Successful Google Advertising Campaigns

B. Vincent

Published by RWG Publishing, 2023.

While every precaution has been taken in the preparation of this book, the publisher assumes no responsibility for errors or omissions, or for damages resulting from the use of the information contained herein.

ADWORDS MASTERY: THE ULTIMATE GUIDE TO SUCCESSFUL GOOGLE ADVERTISING CAMPAIGNS

First edition. April 21, 2023.

Copyright © 2023 B. Vincent.

Written by B. Vincent.

Also by B. Vincent

Affiliate Marketing
Affiliate Marketing
Affiliate Marketing

Standalone
Business Employee Discipline
Affiliate Recruiting
Business Layoffs & Firings
Business and Entrepreneur Guide
Business Remote Workforce
Career Transition
Project Management
Precision Targeting
Professional Development
Strategic Planning
Content Marketing
Imminent List Building
Getting Past GateKeepers
Banner Ads
Bookkeeping
Bridge Pages
Business Acquisition

Business Bogging
Business Communication Course
Marketing Automation
Better Meetings
Business Conflict Resolution
Business Culture Course
Conversion Optimization
Creative Solutions
Employee Recruitment
Startup Capital
Employee Incentives
Employee Mentoring
Followership
Servant Leadership
Human Resources
Team Building
Freelancing
Funnel Building
Geo Targeting
Goal Setting
Immanent List Building
Lead Generation
Leadership Course
Leadership Transition
Leadership vs Management
LinkedIn Ads
LinkedIn Marketing
Messenger Marketing
New Management
Newsfeed Ads
Search Ads
Online Learning
Sales Webinars

- Side Hustles
- Split Testing
- Twitter Timeline Advertising
- Earning Additional Income Through Side Hustles: Begin Earning Money Immediately
- Making a Living Through Blogging: Earn Money Working From Home
- Create Bonuses for Affiliate Marketing: Your Success Is Encompassed by Your Bonuses
- Internet Marketing Success: The Most Effective Traffic-Driving Strategies
- JV Recruiting: Joint Ventures Partnerships and Affiliates
- Secrets to List Building
- Step-by-Step Facebook Marketing: Discover How To Create A Strategy That Will Help You Grow Your Business
- Banner Advertising: Traffic Can Be Boosted by Banner Ads
- Affiliate Marketing
- Improve Your Marketing Strategy with Internet Marketing
- Outsourcing Helps You Save Time and Money
- Choosing the Right Content and Marketing for Social Media
- Make Products That Will Sell
- Launching a Product for Affiliate Marketing
- Pinterest as a Marketing Tool
- Banner Blitz: Mastering the Art of Advertising with Eye-Catching Banners
- Beyond Commissions: Maximizing Affiliate Profits with Creative Bonus Strategies
- Retargeting Mastery: Winning Sales with Online Strategies
- Power Partnerships: Mastering the Art of Business Growth Through Partnership Recruiting
- The List Advantage: Unlocking the Power of List Building for Marketing Success

Capital Catalyst: The Essential Guide to Raising Funds for Your Business
Mobile Mastery: The Ultimate Guide to Successful Mobile Marketing Campaigns
Crowdfunding Secrets: A Comprehensive Guide to Successfully Funding Your Next Project
AdWords Mastery: The Ultimate Guide to Successful Google Advertising Campaigns

Table of Contents

Chapter 1: The Fundamentals of AdWords Advertising 1

Chapter 2: Setting Up Your AdWords Account for Success 5

Chapter 3: Choosing the Right Keywords for Your Campaign 9

Chapter 4: Crafting Effective Ad Copy That Converts 13

Chapter 5: Understanding Ad Rank and Quality Score 17

Chapter 6: Mastering AdWords Bidding Strategies 21

Chapter 7: Building Effective Landing Pages for Your Ads 25

Chapter 8: Targeting the Right Audience with AdWords 29

Chapter 9: Creating Compelling Display Ads that Grab Attention .. 33

Chapter 10: Measuring the Success of Your AdWords Campaigns 37

Chapter 11: Optimizing Your AdWords Campaigns for Maximum ROI 41

Chapter 12: Using AdWords for Branding and Awareness 45

Chapter 13: AdWords for Local Businesses: Tips and Tricks 47

Chapter 14: Creating Effective Remarketing Campaigns 51

Chapter 15: AdWords for eCommerce: Best Practices and Strategies 55

Chapter 16: AdWords for B2B Marketing: Tips and Strategies 59

Chapter 17: AdWords for Lead Generation: Strategies and Tactics ... 63

Chapter 18: Advanced AdWords Techniques: Automation and Machine Learning 67

Chapter 19: Maximizing Your AdWords Budget for Maximum Impact 71

Chapter 20: AdWords and Video Advertising: Best Practices 75

Chapter 21: AdWords and Mobile Advertising: Strategies and Tips. 79

Chapter 22: AdWords for Nonprofits: Maximizing Your Impact 83

Chapter 23: AdWords for Seasonal Campaigns: Tips and Tricks 87

Chapter 24: AdWords and Social Media Advertising: Strategies and Tactics 91

Chapter 25: AdWords in a Changing Landscape: The Future of Google Advertising 95

Chapter 1: The Fundamentals of AdWords Advertising

This chapter is designed for those who are not familiar with AdWords. We will begin by discussing the fundamentals of AdWords, including what it is, how it operates, and what you need to know in order to begin advertising with AdWords.

What exactly is AdWords?

AdWords is Google's online advertising platform that enables businesses to display advertisements on the pages that contain the results of Google searches as well as on other websites that are a part of the Google AdSense program. AdWords is based on a pay-per-click (PPC) model, which means that companies only have to pay when a user clicks on their ad. This allows users to see relevant ads more easily.

How Google AdWords Operates

AdWords is effective because it enables businesses to place bids on particular keywords that are pertinent to the products or services they offer. Google will display ads that are pertinent to a user's search query if the user enters a search query that includes one of the keywords that a company has bid on. These keywords can be found in the business's keyword list. The advertisements are shown both at the top and bottom of the page that contains the search results, in addition to appearing on other websites that are participants in the Google AdSense program.

What You Absolutely Must Be Aware Of

You will need to register for an AdWords account before you can begin advertising with that platform. Providing fundamental information about your company, such as your name, address, and phone number, is all that is required of you to complete this straightforward process.

After you have established your AdWords account, the next step is to develop your initial advertising campaign. A campaign is a series of advertisements that are aimed at reaching a particular demographic of people with the intention of accomplishing a particular objective. You could, for instance, create a campaign with the intention of increasing the number of leads that your company receives, or you could create a campaign with the intention of advertising a particular good or service.

When you are setting up your campaign, one of the steps that you will need to complete is selecting the keywords on which you wish to place bids. It is essential to select keywords that are pertinent to your company and that have a high probability of driving traffic to the website you have in mind.

You will also need to write the copy for your advertisement. Your advertisement's copy needs to be captivating if you want users to engage with it by clicking on it. Include a call-to-action (CTA) in the text of your advertisement. This could be something as simple as "Buy Now" or "Sign Up Today."

At long last, it is time to select the amount of your bid. The amount of your bid is the sum that you are willing to pay for each individual click on your advertisement. You should determine the amount of your bid based on the value that each click brings to your company as well as your available funds.

To sum everything up

AdWords is a potent advertising platform that can assist businesses of any size in expanding their customer base and attracting new clients. In order to get started with AdWords, you will first need to create an account, then your first campaign, then select your keywords, then write your ad copy, and finally choose how much you want to bid. You can create successful AdWords campaigns that generate leads and sales for your company with just a little bit of time and effort on your part. These campaigns will drive traffic to your website.

Chapter 2: Setting Up Your AdWords Account for Success

Setting up your AdWords account properly is the first step in developing a profitable advertising campaign with that platform. In this chapter, we will discuss the most important aspects of establishing a successful foundation for your AdWords account.

Choosing the Right Account Type for You

The selection of your AdWords account type is the initial step in the process of setting up your account. Standard and manager accounts are the two primary classifications of AdWords accounts.

Businesses that want to take control of their own AdWords campaigns will find that a standard account meets their needs. On the other hand, a manager account is ideal for companies that wish to manage multiple AdWords accounts from a single location. This type of account is available to businesses.

Establishing Your Financial Plan

The next step in configuring your AdWords account is to choose a spending limit for your account. The amount of money that you are willing to spend on your AdWords campaign on a daily basis is determined by your budget.

It is essential to create a budget that is suitable for your company and the objectives you wish to achieve. If you are just getting started with AdWords, it is recommended that you begin with a low budget and gradually increase it as you gain experience using the platform. Starting with a low budget will allow you to better gauge the success of your campaigns.

Picking the Right Targeting Method for You

AdWords provides a wide variety of targeting options, allowing you to communicate with the people most likely to be interested in your products or services. The following are some of the most common types of targeting options:

Targeting users who are searching for specific keywords that are relevant to your business gives you the opportunity to focus your marketing efforts on those users.

Targeting users in specific geographic locations, such as cities or countries, is made possible with this feature, which is also known as location targeting.

Targeting users on specific devices, such as desktops, laptops, or mobile devices, is made possible by this feature, which is also referred to as "device targeting."

Targeting users based on specific demographic information, such as age, gender, or income level, is possible thanks to this feature, which is known as demographic targeting.

Putting Together Your Ad Groups

After you have decided which targeting options to use, the next step is to create the ad groups for your campaigns. An advertisement group is a collection of ads that are aimed at a particular keyword or keyword combination.

It is important to choose keywords that are pertinent to your company and that have a good chance of generating traffic to your website when you are creating the ad groups for your advertisements. You should also organize your keywords into themes, as this will allow you to target specific groups of keywords with your advertisements.

Developing the Text of Your Ad

Developing the text for your advertisement is the last step involved in setting up your AdWords account. Your advertisement's copy needs to be captivating if you want users to engage with it by clicking on it.

Your ad copy should include a headline that is clear and concise, a description that highlights the benefits of your product or service, and a call-to-action (CTA) that encourages users to click on your ad. All of these elements should work together to attract users to click on your ad.

It is essential to run multiple experiments with various ad copies in order to determine which advertisements are most successful. You have the ability to create multiple ads within each ad group, and then use the testing tools provided by AdWords to determine which ad copy generates the best results.

To sum everything up

The proper configuration of your AdWords account is absolutely necessary for the production of successful AdWords campaigns. To ensure that your account is properly optimized for performance, you must first select the appropriate account type, then determine your budget, then select your targeting options, then create your ad groups, and finally write persuasive ad copy. You can create AdWords campaigns that drive traffic to your website, which in turn drives leads and sales for your company with a little bit of time and effort invested on your part.

Chapter 3: Choosing the Right Keywords for Your Campaign

It is absolutely necessary to select appropriate keywords in order to build effective AdWords campaigns. In this chapter, we will discuss the most important factors to take into consideration when selecting the appropriate keywords for your AdWords campaign.

Investigation of Keywords

Conducting research on potential keywords is the first thing you need to do before selecting the best keywords for your AdWords campaign. The process of conducting keyword research entails determining the words and phrases that users are entering into search engines in order to find goods or services that are pertinent to your company.

Researching keywords can be accomplished with the assistance of a number of different tools, some of which are the Google Keyword Planner, SEMrush, and Ahrefs. You are able to determine the keywords that are most pertinent to your company by using these tools. Additionally, you are able to determine which keywords have the highest search volume and the least amount of competition.

Choosing Relevant Keywords

After you have finished conducting research on keywords, the next step is to select the keywords that are most pertinent to your company's operations. It is essential to choose keywords that are unique to your company and that have a high probability of driving traffic to your website when you are selecting keywords to use in your marketing efforts.

If you are a plumber, for instance, you might select keywords such as "emergency plumbing services" or "plumbing repairs" to promote your business online. These keywords are highly relevant to your company and have a good chance of attracting website visitors who are looking for plumbing services.

Additionally, it is essential to select keywords that are pertinent to the landing pages that you create. Your ads should be targeting specific keywords, and your landing pages should be designed to correspond with those keywords. This ensures that users have a smooth experience from the moment they click on your ad until the moment they land on your website by providing a seamless transition between the two.

Selecting the Keywords That Have the Appropriate Match Type

AdWords provides a number of match types, each of which enables you to control the degree to which the user's search query needs to correspond with your chosen keyword for your advertisement to be displayed. The following are the four types of matches:

Exact match: Your ad will only be displayed to users whose search queries are an exact match for the keyword that you have selected.

Phrase match means that your advertisement will be displayed when a user's search query contains your chosen keyword in the same order as well as additional words either before or after the phrase.

Broad match means that your advertisement will be displayed whenever a user's search query contains any of the words in your chosen keyword, regardless of the order in which they appear.

Your ad will be displayed when a user's search query contains the words in your chosen keyword, in any order, but with a "+" sign before specific words that must be included in the query. This is referred to as a broad match modifier.

It is vitally important to pick the appropriate type of match if you want your advertisements to be displayed to users who are most likely to be interested in the goods or services that you offer.

Keywords that are not positive

Last but not least, it is essential to select unfavorable keywords. You can think of negative keywords as words or phrases that you do not want to be associated with your advertisements.

For instance, if you run a restaurant that does not serve meat, you might decide to use the word "meat" as a negative keyword. This prevents your advertisements from being shown to users who are conducting a search for eateries that focus on meat.

Choosing negative keywords is an important step to take in order to limit the exposure of your advertisements to only those users who are likely interested in the goods or services you offer.

To sum everything up

It is absolutely necessary to select appropriate keywords in order to build effective AdWords campaigns. Conducting keyword research, selecting keywords with the appropriate match type, selecting relevant keywords, and selecting negative keywords are all necessary steps in the process of selecting the appropriate keywords. You can create AdWords campaigns that drive traffic to your website, which in turn drives leads and sales for your company with a little bit of time and effort invested on your part.

Chapter 4: Crafting Effective Ad Copy That Converts

The development of successful AdWords campaigns begins with the creation of compelling advertisement copy. In this chapter, we will discuss the fundamentals of writing effective advertising copy that converts readers into customers.

Creating Headlines That Are Compelling

When users view your advertisement, the headline is the very first thing that catches their attention. It is essential to compose an enticing headline that immediately grabs the attention of the user and compels them to click on your advertisement.

It is important to remember to include your primary keyword and to emphasize the benefits of your product or service when you are writing the headline for your advertisement. A call-to-action (CTA) that encourages users to click on your ad should also be included in the headline of your advertisement.

Creating Descriptions That Are Interesting To Read

The users will see the headline first, followed by the description of your product. It is important to write an engaging description that highlights the benefits of your product or service and encourages users to click on your ad. This can be accomplished by highlighting the benefits of your product or service.

When you are writing the description of your product or service, it is important to use language that is persuasive and to highlight the features that are unique to your offering. You should also include a call-to-action (CTA) button that prompts users to click on your advertisement.

Implementation of Ad Extensions

Ad extensions are supplemental features that can be added to your advertisements in order to make them more interesting to the target audience and informative. The following are examples of some of the most common ad extensions:

You can include links to specific pages on your website by using sitelink extensions, which allow you to do so.

Callout extensions enable you to draw attention to particular aspects of your product or service, such as its features or advantages.

Structured snippets are a way for you to provide extra information about your products or services, such as the brands or styles that you offer.

Users have a greater chance of clicking on your ad if you make use of ad extensions, which can help to make your ads more interesting and informative for users and increase the likelihood that they will do so.

Conducting Tests on Your Ad Copy

In conclusion, it is essential to conduct tests on your ad copy in order to determine which advertisements are the most successful. AdWords provides a number of testing tools that you can use to evaluate the effectiveness of various versions of your advertisement copy and select the ads that perform the best.

It is important to test one element at a time when you are testing the copy for your advertisement. You could, for instance, test a variety of headlines in order to determine which headline generates the most clicks, and then you could test a variety of descriptions in order to determine which description generates the most clicks.

To sum everything up

The development of successful AdWords campaigns begins with the creation of compelling advertisement copy. In order to craft effective ad copy, you should write headlines that are compelling, write descriptions that are engaging, make use of ad extensions, and test your ad copy to determine which advertisements perform the best. You can create AdWords campaigns that drive traffic to your website, which in turn drives leads and sales for your company with a little bit of time and effort invested on your part.

Chapter 5: Understanding Ad Rank and Quality Score

Both your ad's Ad Rank and Quality Score play a significant role in determining where it will be displayed and how visible it will be within AdWords. In this chapter, we will discuss the most important aspects of Ad Rank and Quality Score, as well as their influence on your AdWords campaigns, and we will do so using examples.

What exactly is the Ad Rank?

The position of your advertisement on a search results page or on a website that is a participant in the Google AdSense program is referred to as the Ad Rank. Your ad's rank is based on a formula that takes into account both the amount you bid and its quality score.

Ad Rank is essential because it decides where your advertisement will be displayed and how visible it will be. Your ad will have a greater chance of being viewed by users in proportion to how high your Ad Rank is.

What exactly does "Quality Score" mean?

Google uses a metric known as Quality Score to evaluate the relevance and quality of your ads and landing pages in order to determine how well they rank. The Quality Score takes into account a number of different aspects, including the following:

The appropriateness of your keywords for your advertisements.

The appropriateness of your advertisements for the landing pages you've provided.

The experience that your landing pages provide for their visitors.

Your AdWords account's performance in the past will be displayed.

Your Ad Rank and the amount that each click on your ads will cost you are directly influenced by your Quality Score. When your Quality Score is higher, your Ad Rank will also be higher, which will result in a lower cost-per-click (CPC).

Increasing Your Overall Score for Quality

There are a number of different things that you can do in order to improve your Quality Score and raise your Ad Rank. These are the following:

Selecting appropriate keywords It is important that you select keywords that are appropriate for your company and that have a good chance of driving traffic to your website.

Ads that are relevant to your keywords and that highlight the benefits of your product or service should be created. Create ads that are relevant to your keywords.

Developing landing pages that are pertinent Develop landing pages that are pertinent to your keywords and advertisements and that provide a positive experience for the user.

Providing a positive experience for the user requires that you check that your landing pages are simple to use, that they load quickly, and that they contain the information that the user is seeking.

Testing and optimizing: Run multiple tests with various iterations of your advertisements and landing pages to determine which versions are most successful. Make use of the data to improve the performance of your ads and landing pages by optimizing them.

To sum everything up

Both your ad's Ad Rank and Quality Score play a significant role in determining where it will be displayed and how visible it will be within AdWords. You should select keywords that are relevant, create ads and landing pages that are relevant, provide a good user experience, test and optimize your campaigns for better performance, and provide a good user experience all in order to improve your Ad Rank and Quality Score. You can create AdWords campaigns that drive traffic to your website, which in turn drives leads and sales for your company with a little bit of time and effort invested on your part.

Chapter 6: Mastering AdWords Bidding Strategies

The amount that you are willing to pay for each click on your ad is determined by your bid, which is an important component of AdWords campaigns because it determines the amount that you are willing to pay. In this chapter, we will discuss the most important aspects of AdWords bidding strategies as well as how to select the strategy that is most appropriate for your company.

Both manual and automated bidding are available.

Manual bidding and automated bidding are the two primary types of bidding strategies that are available through AdWords.

When using manual bidding, you will be able to manually set the amount of your bid for each keyword and ad group. This grants you increased control over your bids, but the management of it will take more time and effort from you.

Automated bidding, on the other hand, enables AdWords to determine the amount of your bid in an automatic manner, taking into account both the goals of your campaign and the data from the past. You may end up saving time and effort as a result of this, but you will have less control over your bids.

How to Determine the Most Appropriate Bidding Strategy

Choosing the optimal bidding strategy is dependent on a number of aspects, such as the objectives of your campaign, the amount of money you have available, and your level of experience using AdWords.

If you are working with a limited budget or are just getting started with Google AdWords, manual bidding may be the most suitable choice for you. Because of this, you will have a greater degree of control over your bids and will be able to make adjustments as necessary.

It's possible that automated bidding is the best choice for you if you have a larger budget, value your time, and want to reduce the amount of work you put in. You may find that using automated bidding helps you achieve your campaign goals in a more efficient and fruitful manner.

Several Distinct Categories of Computerized Bidding Methods

AdWords provides users with access to a variety of automated bidding strategies, including the following:

Target Cost-Per-Acquisition (CPA) Bidding: This feature enables you to establish a desired cost-per-acquisition (CPA) and enables AdWords to adjust your bids so that you can meet your desired CPA.

Target ROAS bidding is a feature that enables you to set a desired return on ad spend (ROAS), and it enables AdWords to adjust your bids so that you can reach that desired ROAS.

Enhanced CPC bidding is a feature that gives AdWords the ability to make real-time adjustments to your bids based on the likelihood that a click will result in a conversion.

Bidding with the Maximize Clicks option enables AdWords to automatically adjust your bids in order to receive the greatest possible number of clicks on your advertisements.

Your level of expertise with AdWords and the goals of your campaign should both be considered when selecting the appropriate automated bidding strategy.

Trying Things Out And Making Adjustments

It is important to test and optimize your bids in order to achieve the best possible results, regardless of the type of bidding strategy that you choose to employ.

You can use the testing and optimization tools provided by AdWords to test out a variety of different bidding strategies and figure out which strategy is the most successful. You can also make changes to your bids based on how well your campaigns are doing, and you can adjust them as necessary.

To sum everything up

The amount that you are willing to pay for each click on your ad is determined by your bid, which is an important component of AdWords campaigns because it determines the amount that you are willing to pay. In order to become an AdWords bidding strategies expert, you must first select the appropriate bidding strategy for your company, then test and optimize your bids, and finally, make adjustments as required. You can create AdWords campaigns that drive traffic to your website, which in turn drives leads and sales for your company with a little bit of time and effort invested on your part.

Chapter 7: Building Effective Landing Pages for Your Ads

It is absolutely necessary to develop landing pages that are efficient in order to convert clicks into leads and sales. In this chapter, we will discuss the essential components that go into making landing pages that are effective for your AdWords ads.

Relevance

Relevance is the first critical component in the construction of efficient landing pages. Your landing pages should have content that is pertinent to both the keywords that you are targeting in your advertisements and the advertisements themselves.

Users have an expectation that when they click on one of your ads, they will be taken to a page that is pertinent to both the search query they entered and the ad that they clicked on. If the user does not find what they are looking for on the landing page that you provide, it is likely that they will navigate away from your website and look elsewhere.

Design

When it comes to turning clicks into leads and sales, the design of your landing pages is just as important as their content. Your landing pages ought to have an appealing aesthetic, an intuitive navigation structure, and a positive impact on the user experience.

Your landing pages should also be optimized for mobile devices, as an increasing number of internet users are accessing the world wide web from their smartphones and other portable electronic devices.

Calls to action that are unmistakable and compelling

The calls-to-action, also known as CTAs, that you include on your landing pages are what motivate users to perform the desired action, such as making a purchase or filling out a form. Your calls to action should be unmistakable, compelling, and simple to locate.

Your calls to action (CTAs) should be consistent with the ads that users clicked on to arrive at your landing page in the first place. If your advertisements promise a particular offer or benefit, then your calls to action (CTAs) should reflect that promise.

Optimization of the Form

It is essential to optimize the forms on any landing pages that contain them in order to achieve the highest possible conversion rate. This means that your forms should be kept as brief and straightforward as is practicable, and that you should only request the information that is absolutely necessary.

In addition to this, you need to make it crystal clear to users what benefits they will derive from completing the form. For instance, if you are giving away a free e-book, you should explain what the book is about and why it is beneficial in as much detail as possible.

Trying Things Out And Making Adjustments

In conclusion, it is essential to perform testing and optimization on your landing pages in order to achieve the highest quality results possible. You can use the testing and optimization tools provided by AdWords to evaluate the performance of various versions of your landing pages and determine which version is most successful.

In addition to this, you should monitor how well your landing pages perform and make adjustments to them as required. This might require you to make some adjustments to the design, copy, or calls to action (CTAs) on your landing pages.

To sum everything up

Converting clicks into leads and sales requires that you build landing pages that are both effective and engaging. In order to construct landing pages that are successful, you need to place a strong emphasis on relevancy, design, calls to action that are both clear and compelling, optimized forms, and testing and optimization. You can create AdWords campaigns that drive traffic to your website, which in turn drives leads and sales for your company with a little bit of time and effort invested on your part.

Chapter 8: Targeting the Right Audience with AdWords

When developing effective AdWords campaigns, it is absolutely necessary to focus on the appropriate audience. In this chapter, we will discuss the most important aspects of using Google AdWords to target the appropriate audience.

Targeting Based on Demographics

AdWords gives you the ability to target your advertisements to specific demographics, including age, gender, and location, amongst others. This gives you the ability to specifically target users who are most likely to be interested in the goods or services that you offer.

For instance, if you own a local company that only provides its services to clients located in a particular region of the country, you can use location targeting to ensure that your advertisements are only viewed by people who live in that region.

Targeting based on one's interests

You can also target your advertisements with AdWords based on the interests of the people you are trying to reach. This gives you the ability to target users who have already demonstrated an interest in subjects that are related to the products or services you offer.

For instance, if you run a store that sells sports equipment, you can use interest-based targeting to communicate with users who have demonstrated an interest in physical activity or competition.

Remarketing

Targeting customers who have already engaged with your brand or website can be accomplished through the use of remarketing, also known as retargeting. This gives you the ability to target users who are already familiar with your brand and who may have a higher propensity to convert as a result.

You could, for instance, use remarketing to target users who have left an incomplete purchase in a shopping cart on your website, with the goal of convincing them to come back and finish making their purchase.

Individualized Target Groups

Targeting users based on specific criteria, such as their email address or phone number, is possible with custom audiences thanks to this feature. This gives you the ability to target users who are already a part of your database and who may have a higher propensity to convert into customers.

For instance, if you have a list of email addresses from customers who have previously made a purchase from your website, you can use custom audiences to target those users with advertisements for new products or services. This is particularly useful if you want to encourage repeat business from those customers.

Trying Things Out And Making Adjustments

Last but not least, in order to get the best possible results from your targeting, it is essential to test it and then optimize it. You can use the testing and optimization tools provided by AdWords to test out the various targeting options available and determine which options provide the best results.

In addition to this, you need to monitor how well your campaigns are doing and adjust them as necessary. This may require making adjustments to your targeting criteria or modifying your bids based on how well your campaigns are performing.

To sum everything up

When developing effective AdWords campaigns, it is absolutely necessary to focus on the appropriate audience. You should concentrate on demographic targeting, interest-based targeting, remarketing, creating custom audiences, and testing and optimizing your content in order to attract the appropriate audience. You can create AdWords campaigns that drive traffic to your website, which in turn drives leads and sales for your company with a little bit of time and effort invested on your part.

Chapter 9: Creating Compelling Display Ads that Grab Attention

It is essential to develop display advertisements that are compelling if you wish to attract the attention of your target audience and to drive traffic to your website. In this chapter, we will discuss the essential components that should be included when developing display advertisements that are captivating.

Design That Draws the Eye

One of the most important aspects that goes into attracting people's attention is the design of your display advertisements. Your advertisements should have a design that is captivating and stands out from the rest of the content that is on the page.

This can be accomplished by utilizing vibrant colors, fonts with a lot of character, as well as high-quality photographs or videos. Your advertisements need to be optimized for a variety of devices, including mobile phones, tablets, and desktop computers.

Messages That Are Both Compelling and Clear

Your display ads' messaging ought to be understandable and compelling to the target audience. You should use language that is convincing, highlighting the benefits of your products or services and encouraging users to take action in response to what they read.

When users click on your advertisement, they will be taken to a landing page. It is important that the messaging on both the ad and the landing page be consistent with one another. If your advertisement makes a certain offer or promises a particular benefit, the landing page that you direct people to should reflect either of these things.

Relevance

Your display advertisements should be pertinent to the interests of the audience you are trying to reach. You should make use of targeting options such as interest-based targeting and remarketing in order to increase the likelihood that users who are most likely to be interested in your products or services will see your advertisements.

Implementation of Ad Extensions

Ad extensions can also be used to create display advertisements that are more engaging. The following are examples of some of the most common ad extensions for display advertisements:

Callout extensions enable you to draw attention to particular aspects of your product or service, such as its features or advantages.

You can include links to specific pages on your website by using site link extensions, which give you this ability.

Review extensions give you the ability to highlight positive reviews or ratings that have been left by customers.

Trying Things Out And Making Adjustments

Last but not least, if you want the best possible results from your display advertisements, it is essential to test and optimize them. You can use the testing and optimization tools provided by AdWords to test out various iterations of your advertisements and determine which iteration yields the best results.

In addition to this, you should monitor how well your advertisements perform and adjust them as required. This may require making adjustments to the layout of your ads, their messaging, or their target audience.

To sum everything up

It is essential to develop display advertisements that are compelling if you wish to attract the attention of your target audience and to drive traffic to your website. Display ads that are compelling are those that have a design that is both eye-catching and compelling, messaging that is both clear and compelling, relevance, the use of ad extensions, and testing and optimization. You can create AdWords campaigns that drive traffic to your website, which in turn drives leads and sales for your company with a little bit of time and effort invested on your part.

Chapter 10: Measuring the Success of Your AdWords Campaigns

It is essential to measure the success of your AdWords campaigns in order to determine whether or not your campaigns are achieving the business goals you have set for yourself. In this chapter, we will discuss the essential components of determining whether or not your AdWords campaigns were successful.

KPIs, also known as Key Performance Indicators

Key performance indicators, also known as KPIs, are metrics that you can use to evaluate how successful your AdWords campaigns have been. The following key performance indicators (KPIs) are among the most important for AdWords campaigns:

Click-through rate, also known as CTR, is the percentage of users who view your advertisements and then click on them after seeing them.

The percentage of users who complete an action that the website owner desires, such as making a purchase or filling out a form, is referred to as the conversion rate.

Cost-per-click (CPC) is a metric that determines how much money you spend on average whenever one of your ads is clicked on.

Return on ad spend, also known as ROAS, is a metric that calculates the amount of revenue produced relative to the amount of money spent on advertising.

Keeping Tabs on Conversions

It is absolutely necessary to track conversions in order to evaluate how successful your AdWords campaigns have been. Conversions are the actions that you want users of your website to take, such as making a purchase or filling out a form. Examples of conversions include filling out a form or making a purchase.

You can track conversions and determine which keywords, ads, and campaigns are producing the most conversions by making use of the conversion tracking tools that are available in AdWords. You can improve the effectiveness of your campaigns by making use of this information and optimizing them.

Analyzing Data

The success of your AdWords campaigns can also be measured by performing data analysis. This is an essential step. You should routinely review the data associated with your campaigns in order to determine which campaigns are successful and which ones could use some tweaking.

You can generate reports on the performance of your campaign using the reporting tools provided by AdWords. These reports can include the performance of individual keywords or ad groups. The decisions you make regarding how to improve the effectiveness of your campaigns can be informed by the data that you get from using this information.

Trying Things Out And Making Adjustments

Last but not least, in order to get the best possible results from your AdWords campaigns, it is essential to test and optimize them. You can use the testing and optimization tools provided by AdWords to test out various iterations of your advertisements and determine which iteration yields the best results.

In addition to this, you should adjust your campaigns so that they better reflect the results of your previous efforts. It's possible that this will require you to make adjustments to your targeting, bids, ad copy, or landing pages.

To sum everything up

It is essential to measure the success of your AdWords campaigns in order to determine whether or not your campaigns are achieving the business goals you have set for yourself. Focusing on key performance indicators, tracking conversions, analyzing data, testing and optimizing ad copy are some of the most important things you can do to evaluate the effectiveness of your AdWords campaigns. You can create AdWords campaigns that drive traffic to your website, which in turn drives leads and sales for your company with a little bit of time and effort invested on your part.

Chapter 11: Optimizing Your AdWords Campaigns for Maximum ROI

It is absolutely necessary to optimize your AdWords campaigns in order to get the most out of your return on investment (ROI). In this chapter, we will discuss the most important aspects of maximizing the return on investment (ROI) from your AdWords campaigns.

Optimization of Search Terms

To ensure that your advertisements are targeting the appropriate keywords, optimization of keywords is an absolute necessity. You should routinely review the data regarding the performance of your keywords in order to identify which keywords are resulting in the highest number of clicks and conversions.

You should also add negative keywords to your campaigns so that your advertisements are not displayed in response to searches that are not relevant to them. Negative keywords are search terms for which you do not want your advertisements to be displayed. These may include terms that are unrelated to the goods or services that you offer.

Optimization of Bids and Offers

In order to maximize your return on investment (ROI), bid optimization is also essential. You need to make it a habit to review your bidding data on a regular basis in order to identify which keywords, ad groups, and campaigns are producing the most conversions.

Automating your bids and achieving the desired return on investment (ROI) can be accomplished with the help of AdWords' automated bidding strategies, such as Target CPA or Target ROAS.

Optimization of the Ad Copy

Optimization of ad copy is essential if you want to make sure that your ads are compelling and relevant to the audience you're trying to reach. You should perform regular reviews of the performance data pertaining to your ad copy in order to identify which ads are producing the highest number of clicks and conversions.

You can use the ad testing tools provided by AdWords to test out various iterations of your ad copy and determine which versions of your ad copy perform the best. When people click on your advertisement, you want to make sure that they are taken to a landing page that is congruent with the ad copy you have written for that advertisement.

Optimization of the Landing Page

The optimization of your landing pages is essential if you want to increase the number of leads and sales that are generated from clicks on those pages. You should routinely review the data regarding the performance of your landing pages in order to determine which landing pages are producing the highest number of conversions.

You can use the landing page testing tools provided by AdWords to evaluate the performance of various versions of your landing pages and determine which version is most successful. You should also make certain that your landing pages are optimized for use on mobile devices and that your calls-to-action are both understandable and compelling.

Trying Things Out And Making Adjustments

Last but not least, in order to get the best possible results from your AdWords campaigns, it is essential to test and optimize them. You should periodically review the data on the performance of your campaign and make adjustments as necessary.

It's possible that this will require you to make adjustments to your targeting, bids, ad copy, or landing pages. You can use the testing and optimization tools provided by AdWords to test various iterations of your campaigns and determine which iterations are the most successful by comparing their performance.

To sum everything up

It is absolutely necessary to optimize your AdWords campaigns in order to maximize your return on investment. To get the most out of your AdWords campaigns, you need to pay close attention to the following aspects: keyword optimization, bid optimization, ad copy optimization, landing page optimization, and testing and optimization. You can create AdWords campaigns that generate traffic to your website, drive leads and sales for your business, and maximize your return on investment (ROI) with just a little bit of time and effort invested in the process.

Chapter 12: Using AdWords for Branding and Awareness

AdWords is a tool that can not only be used to generate traffic and leads, but it can also be used to build recognition and awareness of a brand. In this chapter, we will discuss the most important aspects of using AdWords to build brand awareness and recognition.

Advertisements on Display

Display advertising is one of the most efficient ways to increase both the awareness of and recognition for a brand. Display advertisements are visually appealing and can be designed to include the logo, colors, and messaging of the brand that is being advertised.

You can ensure that users who are likely to be interested in your brand are exposed to your display advertisements by making use of the targeting options provided by AdWords. Some of these options include interest-based targeting and remarketing.

Video Advertising

Advertising via video is another efficient method for increasing both recognition and awareness of a brand. You can use video advertisements to showcase the products or services your brand offers, or you can use them to tell a story about the mission and values your brand upholds.

You can ensure that users who are most likely to be interested in your brand see your video advertisements by making use of the targeting options that are available within AdWords.

Remarketing

Remarketing is a strategy that can also be used to increase recognition and awareness of a brand. Targeting users who have interacted with your brand in the past enables you to maintain your brand's prominence in users' minds and encourages those users to revisit your website and make a purchase there.

You are able to create ads that are specific to users who have previously visited your website or engaged with your brand in some way by utilizing the remarketing tools that are available within AdWords.

Trying Things Out And Making Adjustments

Last but not least, in order to get the best possible results from your branding and awareness campaigns, it is essential to test them and then optimize them. You can use the testing and optimization tools provided by AdWords to test out various iterations of your advertisements and determine which iteration yields the best results.

In addition to this, you need to monitor how well your campaigns are doing and adjust them as necessary. As a result, you might need to make some adjustments to your targeting, messaging, or creative.

To sum everything up

In addition to driving traffic and gathering leads, another purpose that can be served by AdWords is the cultivation of brand awareness and recognition. Display advertising, video advertising, remarketing, testing, and optimization should be the primary focuses of your AdWords efforts if you want to use them to build brand recognition and awareness. You are able to create AdWords campaigns that build brand awareness and recognition for your company with just a little bit of time and effort on your part.

Chapter 13: AdWords for Local Businesses: Tips and Tricks

Local businesses can increase website traffic and lead generation with the help of AdWords, which is a powerful tool. In this chapter, we will discuss the most important hints and recommendations for utilizing AdWords for local companies.

Targeting of Specific Locations

It is essential for local businesses to use location targeting to ensure that their advertisements are displayed to users in their immediate geographic area. You can target users who are located within a certain radius of your business by making use of the location targeting options that are available in AdWords.

You can also target users based on their location if they are searching for keywords that are relevant to your company in the vicinity where your company is located.

Mobile Optimization

Because many users conduct searches for local businesses on their mobile devices, local businesses absolutely need to have their websites optimized for mobile use. You need to check to see that your website is compatible with mobile devices and that your advertisements are formatted appropriately for mobile use.

You can also use the mobile bid adjustments feature in AdWords to increase or decrease your bids for mobile devices depending on the performance of those devices.

Local Ad Extensions

With the help of local ad extensions, you are able to highlight the location of your company as well as its phone number and hours of operation in your advertisements. This can help to raise awareness of your company and encourage users to visit your storefront location in person.

You can add this information to your ads by utilizing the local ad extension options that are available in AdWords. These options include location extensions and call extensions.

Pages d'atterrissage locales

Local landing pages are a useful tool for providing additional information about the location of your business as well as the services it offers. You have the ability to create landing pages that are unique to each location of your business or that are adapted to the community in which your business is situated.

You can also direct users to the landing page that is most relevant to their location by making use of the location-based targeting options that are available within AdWords.

Trying Things Out And Making Adjustments

Last but not least, in order to get the most out of your local AdWords campaigns and get the best possible results, it is essential to test and optimize them. You can use the testing and optimization tools provided by AdWords to test out various iterations of your advertisements and determine which iteration yields the best results.

In addition to this, you need to monitor how well your campaigns are doing and adjust them as necessary. It's possible that this will require you to make adjustments to your targeting, bids, ad copy, or landing pages.

To sum everything up

Local businesses can increase website traffic and lead generation with the help of AdWords, which is a powerful tool. Focusing on location targeting, mobile optimization, local ad extensions, local landing pages, testing and optimization are some of the most important aspects of using AdWords for local businesses. You can create AdWords campaigns that drive traffic to your website, which in turn drives leads and sales for your local company with a little bit of time and effort invested on your part.

Chapter 14: Creating Effective Remarketing Campaigns

Remarketing is a powerful tool that allows you to get back in contact with users who have interacted with your brand in the past. In this chapter, we will discuss the essential components that go into the production of successful remarketing campaigns.

Define Your Target Market for Remarketing

Determining who you will target with your remarketing efforts is the first thing you need to do to create successful campaigns. Users who have interacted with your brand in the past, whether it be through visiting your website, interacting with your brand on social media, or interacting with your brand in some other way, can be used to create remarketing audiences.

You can create these audiences and ensure that your advertisements are shown to users who are most likely to be interested in your brand by utilizing the remarketing tools that are available within AdWords.

Build Your Own Tailored Ads

For remarketing campaigns to be successful, customized ads are an absolute necessity. You should develop advertisements that cater to the specific interests of the audience you are remarketing to and that place an emphasis on the advantages offered by your goods or services.

You can create ads that are unique to each remarketing audience by utilizing the ad customization tools that are available in AdWords. You could, for instance, create advertisements that feature goods or services that the user has previously investigated on your website and use those to target specific audiences.

Set Frequency Caps

The use of frequency caps is absolutely necessary in order to protect your brand by preventing your remarketing audience from seeing your ads an excessive number of times. You need to make sure that you set frequency caps so that your advertisements are not displayed more than a certain number of times on a daily or weekly basis.

This can help to ensure that the audience for your remarketing ads does not perceive your ads as being intrusive or annoying.

Optimize Your Bids

Optimization of your bids is absolutely necessary if you want to make sure that your return on investment (ROI) goals are being met by your remarketing campaigns. You need to make it a habit to review your bidding data on a regular basis in order to determine which remarketing audiences are producing the most conversions and then adjust your bids in accordance with that information.

Automating your bids and achieving the desired return on investment (ROI) can be accomplished with the help of AdWords' automated bidding strategies, such as Target CPA or Target ROAS.

Trying Things Out And Making Adjustments

Last but not least, if you want your remarketing campaigns to produce the best possible results, it is essential to test them and then optimize them. You can use the testing and optimization tools provided by AdWords to test out various iterations of your advertisements and determine which iteration yields the best results.

In addition to this, you need to monitor how well your campaigns are doing and adjust them as necessary. It's possible that this will require you to make some adjustments to your targeting, ad copy, bidding, or frequency caps.

To sum everything up

Remarketing is a powerful tool that allows you to get back in contact with users who have interacted with your brand in the past. You should concentrate on defining your remarketing audience, developing customized advertisements, establishing frequency caps, optimizing your bids, testing and optimizing your campaigns in order to develop successful remarketing initiatives. You can create AdWords campaigns that help your audience feel more connected to your brand and that drive sales and leads for your company with a little bit of time and effort on your part.

Chapter 15: AdWords for eCommerce: Best Practices and Strategies

AdWords is a powerful tool that eCommerce businesses can use to drive traffic and sales to their websites. This chapter will cover some of the most important and useful best practices and strategies for utilizing AdWords for eCommerce.

Product Listing Ads, also known as PLAs

Product Listing Ads, also known as PLAs, are absolutely necessary for online retailers that want to promote their wares within Google's search results. Your product's picture, title, price, and other relevant information are included in its PLA.

You are able to create and manage your PLAs through the use of AdWords' Merchant Center. You need to check that the information about your products is correct and kept up to date so that your product listing ads (PLAs) are displayed to users who are most likely to be interested in the products you sell.

Remarketing That Is Dynamic

eCommerce businesses that want to reconnect with users who have previously interacted with their website can take advantage of a powerful tool called dynamic remarketing. The user's previous activity on your website is tracked and used to personalize the advertisements that are known as dynamic remarketing. These ads feature the goods or services that the user has previously viewed on your website.

You can create these advertisements with the help of AdWords' dynamic remarketing tools, and AdWords will ensure that they are displayed to users who are most likely to be interested in the products you sell.

Shopping Campaigns

E-commerce companies have access to yet another powerful tool in the form of shopping campaigns, which allows them to highlight their products within Google's search results. Shopping campaigns are very similar to PLAs; however, they provide more in-depth information about the products being advertised and are designed to maximize conversions.

Your product advertisements can be crafted and managed with the help of AdWords' Shopping campaigns. If you want your Shopping ads to be displayed to users who are most likely to be interested in the products you sell, you need to make sure that the data associated with your products is accurate and up to date.

Trying Things Out And Making Adjustments

In conclusion, it is essential to run tests and make adjustments to your eCommerce AdWords campaigns in order to get the most accurate and useful results. You can use the testing and optimization tools provided by AdWords to test out various iterations of your advertisements and determine which iteration yields the best results.

In addition to this, you need to monitor how well your campaigns are doing and adjust them as necessary. It's possible that this will require you to make some adjustments to your targeting, ad copy, bids, or product data.

To sum everything up

AdWords is a powerful tool that eCommerce businesses can use to drive traffic and sales to their websites. In order to make the most of AdWords for eCommerce, you need to place a strong emphasis on Product Listing Ads (PLAs), dynamic remarketing, Shopping campaigns, as well as testing and optimization. You can create AdWords campaigns that drive sales for your eCommerce business by investing a little bit of time and effort to create them. These campaigns will generate traffic to your website.

Chapter 16: AdWords for B2B Marketing: Tips and Strategies

AdWords is an effective method for generating leads and sales for businesses that cater to other businesses. In this chapter, we will discuss the most important hints and techniques for using AdWords for business-to-business marketing.

Keyword Targeting

It is essential for businesses that sell to other businesses to use keyword targeting so that their advertisements are displayed to users who are most likely to be interested in the products or services that they offer. You need to concentrate your efforts on targeting keywords that are pertinent to the audience you are trying to reach and that have a high volume of searches.

You can ensure that users who are looking for your products or services will see your ads by utilizing the keyword targeting options that are available in AdWords. Some of these options include exact match and broad match modifier.

Remarketing

Remarketing is also a tool that businesses that sell to other businesses can use to get in touch with users who have visited and interacted with their website in the past. Targeting users who have interacted with your brand in the past enables you to maintain your brand's prominence in users' minds and encourages those users to revisit your website and make a purchase there.

You are able to create ads that are specific to users who have previously visited your website or engaged with your brand in some way by utilizing the remarketing tools that are available within AdWords.

ABM stands for account-based marketing.

Account-Based Marketing, also known as ABM, is an effective method that B2B companies can use to direct their advertisements toward particular accounts or businesses. ABM entails locating high-value accounts or companies and developing personalized advertisements that are catered to the specific requirements and pursuits of the target audience.

You can target these high-value accounts or companies by making use of the targeting options provided by AdWords, such as the company size or industry filters.

Forms for the Generation of Leads

Users who are interested in your goods or services can provide their contact information by filling out lead generation forms, which can be used for this purpose. You have the capability of developing lead generation forms that are uniquely tailored to each of your target audiences or campaigns.

You can add these forms to your ads by utilizing the lead form extensions that are available for AdWords. This will allow your ads to be displayed to users who are most likely to be interested in the products or services that you offer.

Trying Things Out And Making Adjustments

Last but not least, in order to get the most out of your B2B AdWords campaigns and achieve the best possible results, it is essential to test and optimize them. You can use the testing and optimization tools provided by AdWords to test out various iterations of your advertisements and determine which iteration yields the best results.

In addition to this, you need to monitor how well your campaigns are doing and adjust them as necessary. It's possible that this will require you to make some adjustments to your targeting, ad copy, bids, or lead generation forms.

To sum everything up

AdWords is an effective method for generating leads and sales for businesses that cater to other businesses. Keyword targeting, remarketing, Account-Based Marketing (ABM), lead generation forms, testing and optimization are some of the aspects of AdWords that should be emphasized when B2B marketing is being conducted. You can create AdWords campaigns that drive sales and generate leads for your business that caters to other businesses with a little bit of time and effort on your part.

Chapter 17: AdWords for Lead Generation: Strategies and Tactics

AdWords is an effective method for generating leads for your company and is a very powerful tool. In this chapter, we will discuss the most important strategies and approaches for using AdWords as a means of lead generation.

Keyword Targeting

In order to guarantee that users who are most likely to be interested in your goods or services see your advertisements, keyword targeting is an essential component of marketing campaigns designed to generate leads. You need to concentrate your efforts on targeting keywords that are pertinent to the audience you are trying to reach and that have a high volume of searches.

You can ensure that users who are looking for your products or services will see your ads by utilizing the keyword targeting options that are available in AdWords. Some of these options include exact match and broad match modifier.

Forms for the Generation of Leads

Users who are interested in your goods or services can provide their contact information by filling out lead generation forms, which can be used for this purpose. You have the capability of developing lead generation forms that are uniquely tailored to each of your target audiences or campaigns.

You can add these forms to your ads by utilizing the lead form extensions that are available for AdWords. This will allow your ads to be displayed to users who are most likely to be interested in the products or services that you offer.

The acronym "Call-to-Action" (CTA)

It is essential for lead generation campaigns to have a call-to-action (CTA) that is both clear and compelling in order to encourage users to take action. It is recommended that you develop calls to action (CTAs) that are unique to each of your target audiences or campaigns.

You have the ability to create ads in AdWords that include a clear and compelling CTA by utilizing the ad customization tools. Some examples of these types of CTAs include "Download Now" and "Get a Free Quote."

Remarketing

Remarketing is also useful for lead generation campaigns, as it allows users who have interacted with your brand in the past to be reconnected with your company. Targeting users who have interacted with your brand in the past enables you to keep your brand at the forefront of their minds and encourages those users to revisit your website in order to fill out a lead generation form.

You are able to create ads that are specific to users who have previously visited your website or engaged with your brand in some way by utilizing the remarketing tools that are available within AdWords.

Trying Things Out And Making Adjustments

In conclusion, it is essential to conduct tests and make adjustments to your AdWords campaigns if you want to generate the highest quality leads possible. You can use the testing and optimization tools provided by AdWords to test out various iterations of your advertisements and determine which iteration yields the best results.

In addition to this, you need to monitor how well your campaigns are doing and adjust them as necessary. It's possible that this will require you to make adjustments to things like your targeting, ad copy, bidding, lead generation forms, or call-to-action.

To sum everything up

AdWords is an effective method for generating leads for your company and is a very powerful tool. If you want to generate leads with AdWords, you need to pay attention to keyword targeting, lead generation forms, calls to action, remarketing, testing, and optimization. You can build AdWords campaigns that bring in leads and boost sales for your company with a little bit of time and effort on your part.

Chapter 18: Advanced AdWords Techniques: Automation and Machine Learning

AdWords provides a wide variety of cutting-edge methods for automating your campaigns and making use of machine learning to improve the effectiveness of your advertisements. Within the scope of this chapter, we will examine the most important strategies for implementing automation and machine learning within AdWords.

Bidding Methods That Are Computerized

Automated bidding strategies make use of machine learning to make adjustments to your bids based on data collected in real time regarding how well your advertisements are performing. AdWords provides users with a number of automated bidding strategies, such as Target CPA and Target ROAS, which can assist users in achieving the desired return on investment (ROI).

You can improve the performance of your campaigns while simultaneously saving time by utilizing the automated bidding strategies offered by AdWords.

Smart Campaigns

There is a type of AdWords campaign known as "smart campaigns" that makes use of machine learning to automatically optimize your advertisements. AdWords Smart Campaigns are an automated alternative to the manual management of AdWords campaigns for smaller businesses that either lack the time or the expertise to manage their campaigns manually.

The Smart campaign options in AdWords allow you to create campaigns that are automatically optimized for your target audience and the goals you want to achieve.

Dynamic search advertisements

The advertisements that are generated by Dynamic Search Ads are created through the application of machine learning and are based on the content of your website. Businesses that maintain extensive websites with content that is consistently updated are the ideal candidates for Dynamic Search Ads.

You are able to create ads that are automatically generated based on the content of your website by using the Dynamic Search Ad options that are available in AdWords.

Ad Designers and Editors

Ad Customizers make it possible for you to generate advertisements that are uniquely tailored to the user on the basis of real-time information about them, such as their location or the time of day. Ad Customizers are tools that are intended to assist you in developing advertisements that are more pertinent to the audience you are trying to reach.

You have the ability to create ads that are automatically customized based on real-time data about the user by using the Ad Customizer options that are available in AdWords.

Trying Things Out And Making Adjustments

Even when using automation and machine learning, it is critical to test and improve the performance of your AdWords campaigns. You should routinely evaluate how well your campaigns are doing and make adjustments to them as necessary.

You can use the testing and optimization tools provided by AdWords to test out various iterations of your advertisements and determine which iteration yields the best results. You should also monitor how well your campaigns are performing and adapt them as necessary. This could include modifying your targeting, ad copy, or bids, among other things.

To sum everything up

AdWords provides a wide variety of cutting-edge methods for automating your campaigns and making use of machine learning to improve the effectiveness of your advertisements. You should concentrate on using automated bidding strategies, Smart campaigns, Dynamic Search Ads, Ad Customizers, and testing and optimization if you want to use automation and machine learning in AdWords. These are the areas in which you will find the most success. You can create AdWords campaigns that are optimized for your target audience as well as the goals you want to achieve with just a little bit of time and effort.

Chapter 19: Maximizing Your AdWords Budget for Maximum Impact

AdWords has the potential to be an effective tool for driving traffic to your website and increasing sales, but it also has the potential to be expensive. In this chapter, we will discuss the most important strategies for making the most of your AdWords budget in order to achieve the greatest possible impact.

Pay Attention to Keywords With High Value

Focusing on high-value keywords that are likely to generate leads and sales for your company is one of the most important strategies for getting the most out of your AdWords budget. This is one of the most important strategies. You should make use of the keyword research tools that AdWords provides in order to locate keywords that are pertinent to your company and that have a high volume of searches.

You should also put your attention on long-tail keywords, which are less competitive and offer a higher level of specificity. Long-tail keywords may have a lower search volume, but they have the potential to be more targeted and generate leads of a higher quality.

Improve the Performance of Your Landing Pages

Your AdWords campaigns will not be successful without properly utilizing your landing pages. You need to make landing pages that are tailored to each of your different target audiences or campaigns and that are optimized to convert visitors into customers.

Landing pages are web pages that are designed specifically to encourage users to perform a specific action, such as filling out a form to generate leads or making a purchase. In order to provide a satisfying experience for your visitors, you need to make certain that your landing pages are optimized for mobile devices and load quickly.

Keep an Eye on Things and Make Any Necessary Changes to Your Offers

It is essential to regularly monitor and adjust your bids in order to get the most out of your AdWords budget. You need to make sure that your data on bids is reviewed on a regular basis so that you can determine which keywords and campaigns are producing the most sales and leads for your company.

Automating your bids and achieving the desired return on investment (ROI) can be accomplished with the help of AdWords' automated bidding strategies, such as Target CPA or Target ROAS.

Ad Extensions should be used.

Ad extensions are supplemental features that can be added to your advertisements in order to provide users with additional information and encourage them to take some sort of action. Call extensions, location extensions, and sitelink extensions are some of the ad extensions that are available.

To ensure that your ads have the greatest possible impact, you should take advantage of the ad extension options that AdWords provides and add extensions that are both relevant and compelling.

Examine and Improve the Performance of Your Campaigns

Last but not least, in order to get the best possible results from your AdWords campaigns, it is essential to test and optimize them. You can use the testing and optimization tools provided by AdWords to test out various iterations of your advertisements and determine which iteration yields the best results.

In addition to this, you need to monitor how well your campaigns are doing and adjust them as necessary. It's possible that this will require you to make adjustments to your targeting, ad copy, bidding, landing pages, or ad extensions.

To sum everything up

AdWords has the potential to be an effective tool for driving traffic to your website and increasing sales, but it also has the potential to be expensive. You should concentrate on high-value keywords, optimize your landing pages, monitor and adjust your bids, make use of ad extensions, and test and optimize your campaigns in order to get the most out of your AdWords budget and achieve the greatest impact possible. AdWords campaigns can be created to generate leads and drive sales for your company without draining your company's financial resources if you are willing to put in a little bit of time and effort.

Chapter 20: AdWords and Video Advertising: Best Practices

Advertising with videos is an effective method for reaching one's intended demographic and drawing that demographic into interaction with one's brand. AdWords provides users with a number of different options for video advertising, one of which is the use of YouTube Ads. We will discuss the most effective ways to use AdWords for video advertising in this chapter.

Create Compelling Video Content

The production of compelling video content that actively engages your target audience is the first step toward achieving success with video advertising. Your video content should be relevant to your target audience, and it should be designed to tell a story that keeps their attention throughout the entire thing.

Your video content should also be optimized for the platform you are using, such as YouTube or social media, in order to ensure that users have a positive experience when interacting with your brand.

Aim for the Appropriate Audience

It is absolutely essential, for the success of your video advertising campaigns, that you target the appropriate audience. You should make use of the targeting options that are available in AdWords to ensure that users who are most likely to be interested in your products or services are shown your video advertisements.

Your advertisements can be targeted to specific demographics, interests, behaviors, and other factors. Targeting users who have interacted with your brand in the past can also be accomplished with the help of the remarketing tools provided by AdWords.

Make use of the Ad Customizers.

Video advertisements that are uniquely tailored to the user on the basis of real-time data about the user can be crafted with the help of ad customizers. Ad customizers allow you to change the text, images, and calls-to-action in your video advertisements based on the user's location, device, or other data. These changes can be made automatically or manually.

You can create video advertisements that are more pertinent to your target audience by using the ad customizer options that are available in AdWords.

Assess the Performance of Each of Your Campaigns

It is essential to measure the success of your video advertising campaigns if you want to ensure that you are getting the return on investment (ROI) that you want. Tracking the results of your campaigns and adjusting them as necessary should be a priority for you.

You can track metrics such as views, clicks, and conversions by making use of the reporting tools provided by AdWords. In addition to this, you need to conduct an analysis of the performance of your campaigns in order to determine which advertisements and targeting options are the most successful.

Examine and Improve the Performance of Your Campaigns

In conclusion, in order to attain the highest possible levels of success with your video advertising campaigns, it is critical to test and optimize them. You can use the testing and optimization tools provided by

AdWords to test out various iterations of your advertisements and determine which iteration yields the best results.

In addition to this, you need to monitor how well your campaigns are doing and adjust them as necessary. It's possible that this will require you to make some adjustments to your ad's targeting, content, bids, or customizers.

To sum everything up

Advertising with videos is an effective method for reaching one's intended demographic and drawing that demographic into interaction with one's brand. If you want to use AdWords for video advertising, you should focus on creating compelling video content, targeting the appropriate audience, utilizing ad customizers, measuring the success of your campaigns, testing and optimizing your campaigns, and measuring the success of your campaigns. You can create AdWords campaigns that drive sales and generate leads for your company by using video advertising with a little bit of time and effort. These campaigns can be driven by video.

Chapter 21: AdWords and Mobile Advertising: Strategies and Tips

AdWords provides a wide range of options for mobile advertising, which is important because mobile advertising is an essential part of any digital marketing strategy. In this chapter, we will discuss the most important strategies and recommendations for employing AdWords for mobile advertising.

Make sure that your advertisements are optimized for mobile use.

Your advertisements should be optimized for use on mobile devices, as this is one of the most effective strategies for mobile marketing. Your advertisements should take into account the fact that people who use mobile devices behave differently and have different expectations than desktop computer users.

Your advertisements should be designed to be viewable on mobile devices, with messaging that is both clear and succinct, as well as a call-to-action button that is simple to operate on a mobile device. To provide a satisfying experience for your visitors, each of your landing pages ought to be optimized for mobile use.

Aim for the Appropriate Audience

It is absolutely essential, for the success of your mobile advertising campaigns, that you target the appropriate audience. You need to make use of the targeting options that are available in AdWords so that your advertisements are displayed to users who are most likely to be interested in the products or services that you offer.

Your advertisements can be targeted to specific demographics, interests, behaviors, and other factors. Targeting users who have interacted with your brand in the past can also be accomplished with the help of the remarketing tools provided by AdWords.

Ad Extensions should be used.

Ad extensions can be used to provide mobile users with additional information and encourage them to take action by displaying relevant and engaging content. Click-to-call extensions, location extensions, and sitelink extensions are all examples of ad extensions.

If you want your ads to have the greatest possible impact on mobile devices, you should take advantage of the ad extension options that AdWords provides and add extensions that are both relevant and compelling.

Optimisation for local search engine results

Users who are searching from their mobile devices are more likely to be looking for local businesses or services than users who are searching from their desktop computers. You should concentrate on relevant local keywords and incorporate location-based targeting into your mobile advertising campaigns in order to make them more effective for local search.

You should also take advantage of the location extensions that AdWords has to offer in order to give users the address and phone number of your company, thereby making it simpler for them to get in touch with you.

Assess the Performance of Each of Your Campaigns

It is essential to measure the success of your mobile advertising campaigns in order to guarantee that you are achieving the desired return on investment (ROI). Tracking the results of your campaigns and adjusting them as necessary should be a priority for you.

You can track metrics such as clicks, impressions, and conversions by making use of the reporting tools that AdWords provides. In addition to this, you need to conduct an analysis of the performance of your campaigns in order to determine which advertisements and targeting options are the most successful.

Examine and Improve the Performance of Your Campaigns

Last but not least, in order to get the best possible results from your mobile advertising campaigns, it is essential to test them and then optimize them. You can use the testing and optimization tools provided by AdWords to test out various iterations of your advertisements and determine which iteration yields the best results.

In addition to this, you need to monitor how well your campaigns are doing and adjust them as necessary. It's possible that this will require you to make some adjustments to your targeting, ad content, bidding, ad extensions, or landing pages.

To sum everything up

AdWords provides a wide range of options for mobile advertising, which is important because mobile advertising is an essential part of any digital marketing strategy. If you want to use AdWords for mobile advertising, you need to focus on optimizing your ads for mobile devices, targeting the appropriate audience, utilizing ad extensions, optimizing for local search, measuring the success of your campaigns, testing and optimizing your campaigns, and measuring the success of your campaigns. Through mobile advertising, you can create AdWords campaigns that, with a little bit of time and effort on your part, generate leads for your company and drive sales for your company.

Chapter 22: AdWords for Nonprofits: Maximizing Your Impact

AdWords provides a variety of options for nonprofit organizations, allowing them to raise awareness for their cause and communicate with their target audience. In this chapter, we will discuss the most important strategies for maximizing the impact that your use of AdWords for nonprofits can have.

Submissions for Advertising Grants

Google's Ad Grants program is designed to give charitable organizations the opportunity to receive up to $10,000 in free AdWords advertising each month. In addition to meeting the other requirements, your organization needs to be legally recognized as a charitable organization in the country in which you operate in order to be eligible for Ad Grants.

It is essential for nonprofit organizations to apply for Ad Grants as their first step toward maximizing their impact with AdWords. Ad Grants offer free advertising and have the potential to significantly expand your reach.

Develop Advertisement Content That Is Compelling

It is essential to create advertising content that is compelling if you wish to engage your target audience and increase awareness of your cause. Your ad content ought to be designed to be pertinent to your target audience as well as appealing to them, and it ought to include a distinct call to action.

You are able to create ads that are customized based on real-time data about the user, such as their location or the time of day, by using the ad customizers that are available within AdWords.

Aim for the Appropriate Audience

It is absolutely necessary, for the sake of the success of your nonprofit advertising campaigns, to target the appropriate audience. You need to make use of the targeting options that AdWords provides in order to make certain that your advertisements are displayed to users who are most likely to be interested in your cause.

Your advertisements can be targeted to specific demographics, interests, behaviors, and other factors. Targeting users who have interacted with your company in the past can also be accomplished with the help of the remarketing tools provided by AdWords.

Monitor and Evaluate the Effects of Your Actions

It is essential to track and measure your impact in order to ensure that the advertising campaigns your nonprofit is running are successful in achieving the goals you have set for them. You should make use of the reporting tools that AdWords provides in order to keep track of metrics like clicks, impressions, and conversions.

You should also keep track of the impact your campaigns have on your nonprofit organization, such as the number of donations or volunteers they recruit as a result of your campaigns.

Improve the Performance of Your Campaigns

Last but not least, it is essential to make sure that the advertising campaigns you run for your nonprofit organization are optimized so that they produce the best possible results. You can use the testing and optimization tools provided by AdWords to test out various iterations of your advertisements and determine which iteration yields the best results.

In addition to this, you need to monitor how well your campaigns are doing and adjust them as necessary. It's possible that this will require you to make some adjustments to your targeting, ad content, bidding, ad extensions, or landing pages.

To sum everything up

AdWords provides a variety of options for nonprofit organizations, allowing them to raise awareness for their cause and communicate with their target audience. Applying for Ad Grants, developing compelling ad content, targeting the appropriate audience, tracking and measuring your impact, and optimizing your campaigns are all important steps to take if you want to get the most out of AdWords. You can make a significant difference for your charitable organization by utilizing AdWords, provided that you are willing to put in a little bit of time and effort.

Chapter 23: AdWords for Seasonal Campaigns: Tips and Tricks

During times of the year that are marked by holidays, special events, or other seasonal transitions, your company may find that running seasonal campaigns is an effective way to increase traffic and sales. AdWords provides users with a wide range of options for seasonal advertising campaigns. In this chapter, we will discuss the most effective strategies and techniques for utilizing AdWords for seasonal advertising campaigns.

Prepare for the future.

It is absolutely essential to plan ahead in order to ensure the success of seasonal campaigns. You should start planning your campaigns very early on, including the creation of a comprehensive timeline and financial plan.

Researching seasonal trends and behaviors is another step you should take to ensure that your marketing campaigns are directed toward the appropriate audience and address topics that are of interest to them.

Develop Ad Content for the Various Seasons

It is absolutely necessary to develop seasonal advertising content in order to captivate your target audience and pique their interest in your seasonal marketing efforts. Your ad content ought to be designed to be pertinent to your target audience as well as appealing to them, and it ought to include a distinct call to action.

You are able to create ads that are customized based on real-time data about the user, such as their location or the time of day, by using the ad customizers that are available within AdWords.

Aim for the Appropriate Audience

It is absolutely necessary, for the success of your seasonal campaigns, to target the appropriate audience. You need to make use of the targeting options that are available in AdWords to ensure that your seasonal advertisements are displayed to users who are most likely to be interested in them.

Your advertisements can be targeted to specific demographics, interests, behaviors, and other factors. Targeting users who have interacted with your brand in the past can also be accomplished with the help of the remarketing tools provided by AdWords.

Ad Extensions should be used.

Users can be provided with additional information and encouraged to take action by using ad extensions, which can be used to accomplish both of these goals. Call extensions, location extensions, and sitelink extensions are some of the ad extensions that are available.

If you want your ads to have the greatest possible impact on seasonal campaigns, you should take advantage of the ad extension options that AdWords provides and add extensions that are both relevant and compelling.

Monitor and Evaluate the Effects of Your Actions

It is essential to track and measure your impact in order to guarantee that your seasonal campaigns are successful in achieving the objectives you have set for them. You should make use of the reporting tools that AdWords provides in order to keep track of metrics like clicks, impressions, and conversions.

You should also monitor the effect that your campaigns have on your company's overall performance, such as the total number of sales or leads they produce.

Improve the Performance of Your Campaigns

Last but not least, it is essential to perfect your seasonal marketing campaigns in order to get the most effective outcomes. You can use the testing and optimization tools provided by AdWords to test out various iterations of your advertisements and determine which iteration yields the best results.

In addition to this, you need to monitor how well your campaigns are doing and adjust them as necessary. It's possible that this will require you to make some adjustments to your targeting, ad content, bidding, ad extensions, or landing pages.

To sum everything up

Seasonal marketing campaigns have the potential to be an effective tool for driving traffic to your website and increasing sales. Planning ahead, developing seasonal ad content, targeting the appropriate audience, making use of ad extensions, tracking and measuring your impact, and optimizing your campaigns are all necessary steps for using AdWords for seasonal marketing campaigns. You are able to create AdWords campaigns that will generate leads and drive sales for your company during seasonal periods by investing a small amount of time and effort into the process.

Chapter 24: AdWords and Social Media Advertising: Strategies and Tactics

Advertising on social media platforms is an effective method for reaching one's intended demographic and drawing that demographic into interaction with one's brand. AdWords provides users with a number of different options for advertising on social media platforms, including choices for advertising on social media platforms such as Facebook and Instagram, amongst others. In this chapter, we will discuss the most effective strategies and procedures for utilizing AdWords for advertising on social media platforms.

Develop Advertisement Content That Is Compelling

The first thing you need to do to ensure your advertising campaign on social media is successful is to develop compelling content for your ads that will engage the people you want to reach. Your ad's content needs to be relevant to the people you're trying to reach, and it also needs to be structured to tell a story that draws people in and holds their attention.

Your advertising content should also be optimized for the platform that you are using, such as Facebook or Instagram, in order to provide users with a satisfying experience overall.

Aim for the Appropriate Audience

In order for your advertising campaigns on social media to be successful, it is essential that you target the appropriate audience. You need to make use of the targeting options that are available in AdWords so that your advertisements are displayed to users who are most likely to be interested in the products or services that you offer.

Your advertisements can be targeted to specific demographics, interests, behaviors, and other factors. Targeting users who have interacted with your brand in the past can also be accomplished with the help of the remarketing tools provided by AdWords.

Make use of the Ad Customizers.

Ad customizers can be used to create social media ads that are customized based on real-time data about the user. These ads can then be published on the social media platform. Ad customizers allow you to alter the text, images, and calls-to-action in your social media ads based on the location of the user, the device they are using, or any other data that you provide.

You can create social media ads that are more relevant to your target audience by using the ad customizer options that are available within AdWords.

Assess the Performance of Each of Your Campaigns

It is essential to measure the success of your advertising campaigns on social media in order to ensure that you are achieving the desired return on investment (ROI). Tracking the results of your campaigns and adjusting them as necessary should be a priority for you.

You can track metrics such as views, clicks, and conversions by making use of the reporting tools provided by AdWords. In addition to this, you need to conduct an analysis of the performance of your campaigns in order to determine which advertisements and targeting options are the most successful.

Examine and Improve the Performance of Your Campaigns

Last but not least, in order to get the best possible results from your advertising campaigns on social media, it is essential to test them and then optimize them. You can use the testing and optimization tools provided by AdWords to test out various iterations of your advertisements and determine which iteration yields the best results.

In addition to this, you need to monitor how well your campaigns are doing and adjust them as necessary. It's possible that this will require you to make some adjustments to your ad's targeting, content, bids, or customizers.

To sum everything up

Advertising on social media platforms is an effective method for reaching one's intended demographic and drawing that demographic into interaction with one's brand. If you want to use AdWords for advertising on social media, you should concentrate on creating compelling ad content, targeting the appropriate audience, utilizing ad customizers, measuring the success of your campaigns, testing and optimizing your campaigns, and measuring the success of your campaigns. Through the use of social media advertising, you can create AdWords campaigns that, with just a little bit of time and effort on your part, generate leads for your company and drive sales.

Chapter 25: AdWords in a Changing Landscape: The Future of Google Advertising

Google AdWords has been a critical tool for digital marketers for many years, but the landscape of online advertising is constantly evolving. In this chapter, we will explore the future of Google advertising and what changes we can expect to see in the coming years.

Machine Learning and Automation

One of the most significant trends in Google advertising is the increasing use of machine learning and automation. Google is investing heavily in machine learning technology to improve ad targeting, ad delivery, and ad performance.

In the future, we can expect to see more automation in the management of AdWords campaigns, with less manual intervention required. This will enable advertisers to focus more on strategy and creativity, while allowing Google to handle the more mundane tasks.

Integration with Other Platforms

Another trend we can expect to see in the future of Google advertising is increased integration with other platforms. Google is looking to make it easier for advertisers to manage their advertising across multiple platforms, such as YouTube and Google Maps.

In the future, we can expect to see more cross-platform advertising options and improved tools for managing advertising campaigns across multiple platforms.

Privacy and Data Protection

Privacy and data protection are increasingly important concerns for consumers and regulators alike. In response to these concerns, Google is taking steps to improve privacy and data protection for its users.

In the future, we can expect to see more emphasis on user privacy and data protection in Google advertising. This may include changes to the way user data is collected and used, as well as increased transparency around data collection and use.

New Ad Formats

Google is constantly experimenting with new ad formats to improve user engagement and ad performance. In the future, we can expect to see more new ad formats, such as interactive ads, augmented reality ads, and voice-activated ads.

These new ad formats will offer advertisers new opportunities to engage with their target audience and provide more immersive and interactive advertising experiences.

Conclusion

Google AdWords has been a critical tool for digital marketers for many years, but the landscape of online advertising is constantly evolving. The future of Google advertising will be shaped by trends such as machine learning and automation, integration with other platforms, privacy and data protection, and new ad formats.

As the advertising landscape continues to evolve, it is important for digital marketers to stay informed and adapt their strategies accordingly. By keeping up with the latest trends and developments in Google advertising, marketers can stay ahead of the competition and drive results for their business.

Also by B. Vincent

Affiliate Marketing
Affiliate Marketing
Affiliate Marketing

Standalone
Business Employee Discipline
Affiliate Recruiting
Business Layoffs & Firings
Business and Entrepreneur Guide
Business Remote Workforce
Career Transition
Project Management
Precision Targeting
Professional Development
Strategic Planning
Content Marketing
Imminent List Building
Getting Past GateKeepers
Banner Ads
Bookkeeping
Bridge Pages
Business Acquisition

Business Bogging
Business Communication Course
Marketing Automation
Better Meetings
Business Conflict Resolution
Business Culture Course
Conversion Optimization
Creative Solutions
Employee Recruitment
Startup Capital
Employee Incentives
Employee Mentoring
Followership
Servant Leadership
Human Resources
Team Building
Freelancing
Funnel Building
Geo Targeting
Goal Setting
Immanent List Building
Lead Generation
Leadership Course
Leadership Transition
Leadership vs Management
LinkedIn Ads
LinkedIn Marketing
Messenger Marketing
New Management
Newsfeed Ads
Search Ads
Online Learning
Sales Webinars

Side Hustles
Split Testing
Twitter Timeline Advertising
Earning Additional Income Through Side Hustles: Begin Earning Money Immediately
Making a Living Through Blogging: Earn Money Working From Home
Create Bonuses for Affiliate Marketing: Your Success Is Encompassed by Your Bonuses
Internet Marketing Success: The Most Effective Traffic-Driving Strategies
JV Recruiting: Joint Ventures Partnerships and Affiliates
Secrets to List Building
Step-by-Step Facebook Marketing: Discover How To Create A Strategy That Will Help You Grow Your Business
Banner Advertising: Traffic Can Be Boosted by Banner Ads
Affiliate Marketing
Improve Your Marketing Strategy with Internet Marketing
Outsourcing Helps You Save Time and Money
Choosing the Right Content and Marketing for Social Media
Make Products That Will Sell
Launching a Product for Affiliate Marketing
Pinterest as a Marketing Tool
Banner Blitz: Mastering the Art of Advertising with Eye-Catching Banners
Beyond Commissions: Maximizing Affiliate Profits with Creative Bonus Strategies
Retargeting Mastery: Winning Sales with Online Strategies
Power Partnerships: Mastering the Art of Business Growth Through Partnership Recruiting
The List Advantage: Unlocking the Power of List Building for Marketing Success

Capital Catalyst: The Essential Guide to Raising Funds for Your Business

Mobile Mastery: The Ultimate Guide to Successful Mobile Marketing Campaigns

Crowdfunding Secrets: A Comprehensive Guide to Successfully Funding Your Next Project

AdWords Mastery: The Ultimate Guide to Successful Google Advertising Campaigns

About the Publisher

Accepting manuscripts in the most categories. We love to help people get their words available to the world.

Revival Waves of Glory focus is to provide more options to be published. We do traditional paperbacks, hardcovers, audio books and ebooks all over the world. A traditional royalty-based publisher that offers self-publishing options, Revival Waves provides a very author friendly and transparent publishing process, with President Bill Vincent involved in the full process of your book. Send us your manuscript and we will contact you as soon as possible.

Contact: Bill Vincent at rwgpublishing@yahoo.com

www.ingramcontent.com/pod-product-compliance
Lightning Source LLC
LaVergne TN
LVHW011727060526
838200LV00051B/3051